C000162715

summersdale

I LOVE YOU

An Hachette UK Company
www.hachette.co.uk

Summersdale Publishers Ltd
Part of Octopus Publishing Group Limited
Carmelite House
50 Victoria Embankment
LONDON
EC4Y 0DZ
UK

www.summersdale.com

Printed and bound in China

ISBN: 978-1-78783-580-1

Substantial discounts on bulk quantities of Summersdale books are available to corporations, professional associations and other organizations. For details contact general enquiries: telephone: +44 (0) 1243 771107 or email: enquiries@summersdale.com.

TO.............................

FROM.....................

IF I DO
NOT LOVE
YOU I SHALL
NOT LOVE.

SAMUEL BECKETT

ALL YOU NEED
IN THE WORLD IS
LOVE AND LAUGHTER.
THAT'S ALL
ANYBODY NEEDS.

AUGUST WILSON

WHAT IS ALL
THIS SWEET
WORK WORTH
IF THOU KISS
NOT ME?

PERCY BYSSHE SHELLEY

I AM ONE OF THOSE BEINGS FORMED BY NATURE FOR ROMANCE.

ELLEN JOHNSTON

WHAT GREATER
THING IS THERE
FOR TWO
HUMAN SOULS,
THAN TO FEEL
THAT THEY ARE
JOINED FOR LIFE?

GEORGE ELIOT

BEING WITH YOU IS BETTER THAN A DREAM

LET US ROLL ALL OUR STRENGTH AND ALL OUR SWEETNESS UP INTO ONE BALL.

ANDREW MARVELL

I feel
IN MY INMOST
heart your admirable
qualities
AND
feelings.

EMMA DARWIN

Every kiss is true love's kiss

MY EYES HOLD HER!
WHAT IS WORTH
THE REST OF HEAVEN,
THE REST OF EARTH?

ROBERT BROWNING

YOU DON'T LOVE
SOMEONE BECAUSE
THEY'RE PERFECT.
YOU LOVE THEM IN
SPITE OF THE FACT
THEY'RE NOT.

JODI PICOULT

EVERYTHING
IS CLEARER
WHEN YOU'RE
IN LOVE.

JOHN LENNON

You're my favourite EVERYTHING

THOU HAST POSSESSED
THYSELF OF MY HEART;
THOU HAS FIXED
THY ABODE IN IT.

ANTARAH IBN SHADDAD

THE BIRTHDAY
OF MY LIFE
IS COME,
MY LOVE IS
COME TO ME.

Christina Rossetti

IT TOOK
ONLY A
HEART-
BEAT
TO FALL
FOR YOU

YOU ALWAYS
GAIN BY
GIVING LOVE.

REESE WITHERSPOON

I want
NOTHING
from love,
IN SHORT,
but love.

COLETTE

THE SUBJECT TONIGHT IS LOVE AND FOR TOMORROW NIGHT AS WELL.

HAFIZ

TO LOVE ANOTHER
IS SOMETHING
LIKE PRAYER...
YOU JUST FALL
INTO ITS ARMS
BECAUSE YOUR
BELIEF UNDOES
YOUR DISBELIEF.

ANNE SEXTON

ONE MUST LOVE
HUMANITY IN ORDER
TO REACH OUT INTO
THE UNIQUE
ESSENCE OF EACH
INDIVIDUAL.

GEORG BÜCHNER

My LOVE language is YOU

I CANNOT SAY
WHAT LOVES HAVE
COME AND GONE,
I ONLY KNOW
THAT SUMMER
SANG IN ME.

EDNA ST VINCENT MILLAY

LOVE DOESN'T
JUST SIT THERE,
LIKE A STONE,
IT HAS TO BE
MADE, LIKE
BREAD; REMADE
ALL THE TIME,
MADE NEW.

Ursula K. Le Guin

BEAUTY IS NOT
IN THE FACE;
BEAUTY IS
A LIGHT IN
THE HEART.

KAHLIL GIBRAN

YOUR
LOVE
PROVES
MIRACLES
EXIST

YOU LIE IN
ALL MY MANY
THOUGHTS,
LIKE LIGHT,
LIKE THE FAIR
LIGHT OF DAWN.

SAMUEL TAYLOR COLERIDGE

I LOVE AND AM LOVED, FULLY AND FREELY, NOTHING EXPECTED, MORE THAN ENOUGH RECEIVED.

AMY TAN

WHEN YOU'RE LUCKY ENOUGH TO MEET YOUR ONE PERSON, THEN LIFE TAKES A TURN FOR THE BEST. IT CAN'T GET BETTER THAN THAT.

JOHN KRASINSKI

Love
WAS
the great
AND
beautiful
wonder.

SUSAN GLASPELL

LOVE WITHOUT
FRIENDSHIP IS
LIKE A SHADOW
WITHOUT THE SUN.

JAPANESE PROVERB

You're the **ONLY PERSON** I'd share my food with

TO BE BRAVE
IS TO LOVE
SOMEONE
UNCONDITIONALLY,
WITHOUT
EXPECTING
ANYTHING
IN RETURN.

MADONNA

SOMETIMES
YOU WIN THE
TRIPLE CROWN:
GOOD FOOD,
GOOD SEX AND
GOOD TALK.

TONI MORRISON

WHEREVER
IN THE
WORLD
I AM, MY
HEART IS
WITH YOU

THERE'S NO
SUBSTITUTE FOR
A GREAT LOVE
WHO SAYS,
"NO MATTER WHAT'S
WRONG WITH YOU,
YOU'RE WELCOME AT
THIS TABLE."

TOM HANKS

NATURE CRAVES LOVE.

DANTE ALIGHIERI

IT'S ABOUT BEING
COMMITTED ENOUGH
AND LOVING YOUR
PARTNER ENOUGH
TO HANG IN THERE
REGARDLESS.

CANDACE CAMERON BURE

You're my
ADVENTURE
and my
PEACE

LIFE AND LOVE
ARE VERY
PRECIOUS
WHEN BOTH
ARE IN FULL
BLOOM.

Louisa May Alcott

YOU MAY
make love
in dancing
AS WELL AS
sitting.

APHRA BEHN

I DESIRE

THEREFORE

I EXIST.

ANGELA CARTER

TRUE LOVE
IS A DURABLE
FIRE IN THE
MIND EVER
BURNING.

WALTER RALEIGH

OPEN YOUR HEART
TO THE WONDER
OF DREAMS AND
MOONLIGHT.

AUGUSTA HOLMÈS

You're
MY
person

LOVE IS A
DECISION,
NOT JUST AN
EMOTION.
IT IS SELFLESS,
AND A
COMMITMENT.

Lydia McLaughlin

THE ESSENTIAL CONDITIONS OF EVERYTHING YOU DO MUST BE CHOICE, LOVE, PASSION.

NADIA BOULANGER

YOU HAVE
ALL OF MY
HEART

LOVE IS
lak de sea.
IT'S UH
movin' thing,
BUT
still and all.

ZORA NEALE HURSTON

I HAVE NO
JOYS THAT ARE
NOT YOURS, NO
ACHES WHICH
ARE NOT YOURS.

KAMALA DAS

IF I WERE LOVED,
AS I DESIRE TO BE,
WHAT IS THERE
IN THIS GREAT
SPHERE OF EARTH,
AND RANGE OF
EVIL BETWEEN
DEATH AND
BIRTH, THAT I
SHOULD FEAR...?

ALFRED TENNYSON

You
make my
HEART
skip a
BEAT

YOURS, MY LOVE,
IS THE RIGHT
HUMAN FACE.
I IN MY MIND
HAD WAITED FOR
THIS LONG.

EDWIN MUIR

THERE IS ALWAYS
SOMETHING
LEFT TO LOVE.
AND IF YOU
AIN'T LEARNED
THAT, YOU
AIN'T LEARNED
NOTHING.

LORRAINE HANSBERRY

IT'S
IMPOSSIBLE TO
BE *BORED*
WHEN I'M
WITH *YOU*

You can't
DESCRIBE
someone
YOU'RE IN
love with!

TENNESSEE WILLIAMS

I BELIEVE IN
THE RELIGION
OF LOVE,
WHATEVER
DIRECTION ITS
CARAVANS
MAY TAKE.

IBN ARABI

Everything changed when I met you

SO MANY
THINGS I WOULD
GIVE YOU HAD
I AN INFINITE
GREAT STORE.

EDWARD THOMAS

BEING IN LOVE
SHOWS A PERSON
WHO THEY
SHOULD BE.

ANTON CHEKHOV

THEY SHALL
BE ONE FLESH,
ONE HEART,
ONE SOUL.

JOHN MILTON

Lover,
let me
HOLD
you in my
ARMS

JUST LOVE EACH
OTHER, LAVISH
EACH OTHER
WITH LOVE.

NICOLE KIDMAN

WE CAN ONLY
LEARN TO LOVE
BY LOVING.

IRIS MURDOCH

Light
OF MY
dark,
BLOOD OF MY
heart.

FRANCIS THOMPSON

I LOVE
THE LIFE
WE'RE
BUILDING
TOGETHER

ALL MUST
FALL IN LOVE
WITH THE
SIGHT OF
YOUR EYES.

AL-MUTANABBI

A TRUE SOULMATE IS A MIRROR.

ELIZABETH GILBERT

My LOVE
is TRUE
to my
TRUE LOVE

THE WORLD IS
LITTLE, PEOPLE
ARE LITTLE,
HUMAN LIFE IS
LITTLE. THERE
IS ONLY ONE BIG
THING – DESIRE.

WILLA CATHER

COULD I
EVER HAVE
LOVED YOU,
HAD I NOT
KNOWN YOU
BETTER THAN
YOU KNOW
YOURSELF?

HARRIET BEECHER STOWE

WHEN YOU FIND
THAT ONE THAT'S
RIGHT FOR YOU,
YOU FEEL LIKE
THEY WERE PUT
THERE FOR YOU.

JOE MANGANIELLO

You
are my
SWEETHEART

WHENEVER WE CAN
MANAGE TO LOVE
WITHOUT EXPECTATIONS,
CALCULATIONS,
NEGOTIATIONS, WE ARE
INDEED IN HEAVEN.

RUMI

I LOVED
HIM FOR HIMSELF
ALONE.

RICHARD BRINSLEY SHERIDAN

WE ARE
TWO
HALVES
OF ONE
WHOLE

I DO NOT
WANT HORSES
OR DIAMONDS
— I AM HAPPY
IN POSSESSING
YOU.

CLARA SCHUMANN

IF YOU ARE NOT IN LOVE, HOW CAN YOU ENJOY THE BLINDING LIGHT OF THE SUN, THE SOFT LIGHT OF THE MOON?

OMAR KHAYYAM

Perhaps
WE ARE
in this world
TO SEARCH
for love.

ISABEL ALLENDE

WERE I
WITH THEE
WILD NIGHTS
SHOULD BE
OUR LUXURY!

EMILY DICKINSON

I SAW
CLEARLY ONLY
WHEN I SAW
WITH LOVE.

ARTHUR MILLER

There's
no one in
the WORLD
like YOU

I UTTER SIGHS,
IN CALLING
OUT TO YOU,
WITH THE
NAME THAT
LOVE WROTE
ON MY HEART.

PETRARCH

I fell in love
THE WAY YOU
fall asleep:
SLOWLY,
AND THEN
all at once.

JOHN GREEN

TRUE LOVE
ALWAYS MAKES
A MAN BETTER.

ALEXANDRE DUMAS

SO I, AS I GROW
STIFF AND COLD
TO THIS AND THAT
SAY GOOD-BYE TOO;
AND EVERYBODY SEES
THAT I AM OLD
BUT YOU.

CHARLOTTE MEW

IF EVER
TWO WERE
ONE, THEN
SURELY WE.

ANNE BRADSTREET

Your
LOVE
is
MAGIC

ONE WORD
FREES US
OF ALL THE
WEIGHT AND
PAIN OF LIFE:
THAT WORD
IS LOVE.

SOPHOCLES

IF YOU ONLY
KNEW HOW
MY HEART
BEATS WHEN
I THINK
OF YOU.

ANGELINA WELD GRIMKÉ

To love,
OR TO HAVE
loved,
IS
enough.

VICTOR HUGO

LOVE IS
SOMETHING
ETERNAL;
THE ASPECT
MAY CHANGE,
BUT NOT THE
ESSENCE.

Vincent van Gogh

A KISS IS A
LOVELY TRICK
DESIGNED BY
NATURE TO STOP
SPEECH WHEN
WORDS BECOME
SUPERFLUOUS.

INGRID BERGMAN

There are no ACCIDENTAL meetings between SOULS

LOVE IS THE
ONE THING
STRONGER
THAN DESIRE
AND THE ONLY
PROPER REASON
TO RESIST
TEMPTATION.

JEANETTE WINTERSON

Kiss me,
AND YOU
will see how
important
I am.

SYLVIA PLATH

LOVE BRINGS
LIGHT TO A
LOVER'S NOBLE
AND HIDDEN
QUALITIES —
HIS RARE AND
EXCEPTIONAL
TRAITS.

FRIEDRICH NIETZSCHE

MY LOVE IS
SUCH THAT RIVERS
CANNOT QUENCH.

ANNE BRADSTREET

I LOVE THEE
WITH THE BREATH,
SMILES, TEARS,
OF ALL MY LIFE.

ELIZABETH BARRETT BROWNING

I'm
CRAZY
about
YOU

WE LOVE
BECAUSE IT IS
THE ONLY TRUE
ADVENTURE.

NIKKI GIOVANNI

**LET YOUR LOVE
BE LIKE THE
MISTY RAINS,
COMING SOFTLY,
BUT FLOODING
THE RIVER.**

MALAGASY PROVERB

IF YOU REMEMBER
ME, THEN I DON'T
CARE IF EVERYONE
ELSE FORGETS.

HARUKI MURAKAMI

I COULD SPEND

ETERNITY

IN YOUR

ARMS

ROMANCE IS
THE GLAMOUR
WHICH TURNS
THE DUST
OF EVERYDAY
LIFE INTO A
GOLDEN HAZE.

Elinor Glyn

I WANT YOU.
I WANT YOU
HUNGRILY,
FRENZIEDLY,
PASSIONATELY.
I AM STARVING
FOR YOU.

VIOLET TREFUSIS

You've changed my LiFE for the BETTER

LOVE IS
FRIENDSHIP
SET ON FIRE.

JEREMY TAYLOR

ROMANCE IS EVERYTHING.

GERTRUDE STEIN

O HEART
O LOVE
EVERYTHING
IS SUDDENLY
TURNED TO
GOLD!

ALLEN GINSBERG

YOU ARE THE
LOVELIEST
BEING ON THIS
EARTH

YOU KNOW IT'S
LOVE WHEN ALL
YOU WANT IS
THAT PERSON TO
BE HAPPY, EVEN
IF YOU'RE NOT
PART OF THEIR
HAPPINESS.

Julia Roberts

Love

IS A CANVAS

furnished by

Nature

AND EMBROIDERED BY

imagination.

VOLTAIRE

WHEN I SAW YOU I FELL IN LOVE, AND YOU SMILED BECAUSE YOU KNEW.

ARRIGO BOITO

LOVE IS
THE EMBLEM
OF ETERNITY.

MADAME DE STAËL

I WANT TO
PUT MY ARMS
AROUND YOU.
I ACHE TO HOLD
YOU CLOSE.

ELEANOR ROOSEVELT

I can't
WAIT for
tomorrow
with
YOU

IN DREAMS
AND IN LOVE
THERE ARE NO
IMPOSSIBILITIES.

JÁNOS ARANY

WHEN
YOU LOVE
SOMEONE,
ALL YOUR
SAVED-UP
WISHES START
COMING OUT.

ELIZABETH BOWEN

YOU'RE THE LIGHT IN EVEN MY DARKEST TIMES

YOUR LIPS
BRING
BLESSINGS.

MARGARET MEAD

YOU ARE
always new.
THE LAST OF
your kisses
WAS EVER
the sweetest.

JOHN KEATS

NOTHING WILL
MATTER BUT JUST
WE TWO, WE TWO
LONGING LOVES AT
LAST COME TOGETHER.

RADCLYFFE HALL

THE WINDS WERE
WARM ABOUT US,
THE WHOLE EARTH
SEEMED THE
WEALTHIER FOR
OUR LOVE.

HARRIET ELIZABETH
PRESCOTT SPOFFORD

I WAKE UP
EVERY MORNING
THANKFUL THAT
IT WASN'T ALL
A DREAM.

ADAM LEVINE

YOU are my BEST FRIEND

A HEART THAT
LOVES IS
ALWAYS YOUNG.

GREEK PROVERB

IF MUSIC BE THE
FOOD OF LOVE,
PLAY ON.

WILLIAM SHAKESPEARE

WITHOUT LOVE, THE WORLD ITSELF WOULD NOT SURVIVE.

LOPE DE VEGA

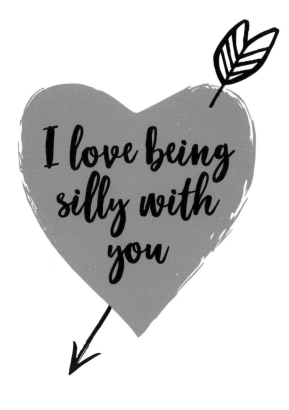

Love
CAN TURN A
cottage
INTO A
golden palace.

GERMAN PROVERB

**MY HEART HAS
MADE ITS MIND UP
AND I'M AFRAID
IT'S YOU.**

WENDY COPE

I WANT to hold your HAND

IT'S THE KIND
OF KISS THAT
INSPIRES STARS
TO CLIMB INTO
THE SKY AND
LIGHT UP
THE WORLD.

TAHEREH MAFI

EACH TIME YOU HAPPEN TO ME ALL OVER AGAIN.

EDITH WHARTON

IT IS A
WONDERFUL
SEASONING OF
ALL ENJOYMENTS
TO THINK OF
THOSE WE LOVE.

MOLIÈRE

WE DON'T
EVEN HAVE TO
SPEAK
TO UNDERSTAND
EACH OTHER

**TO WINE,
TO OPIUM EVEN,
I PREFER THE
ELIXIR OF YOUR LIPS
ON WHICH LOVE
FLAUNTS ITSELF.**

CHARLES BAUDELAIRE

THE HEART
IS AN ORGAN
OF FIRE.

MICHAEL ONDAATJE

My sweetest
DREAMS
are of
YOU

COME LIVE
WITH ME AND
BE MY LOVE.

CHRISTOPHER MARLOWE

I SAW SOMEBODY
AND EXPERIENCED
ALL OF THOSE
THINGS YOU HEAR
ABOUT IN SONGS
AND READ ABOUT
IN POETRY. MY
KNEES WERE WEAK.

PORTIA DE ROSSI

YES, LOVE
SHALL WIN!

HENRIK IBSEN

WILL YOU COME
TRAVEL WITH ME?
SHALL WE STICK
BY EACH OTHER
AS LONG AS
WE LIVE?

WALT WHITMAN

If you're interested in finding out more about our books, find us on Facebook at **SUMMERSDALE PUBLISHERS** and follow us on Twitter at **@SUMMERSDALE**.

WWW.SUMMERSDALE.COM

IMAGE CREDITS